Hawks on Wires

Hawks on Wires

Poems, 2005–2010

Dave Smith

stīg under læg
eldum uncn̄ð
—*Beowulf,* II, 2213–2214

gold eyes, unforgiving, for they, like God, see all . . .
—ROBERT PENN WARREN

Louisiana State University Press
Baton Rouge

Published by Louisiana State University Press
Manufactured in the United States of America
FIRST PRINTING

DESIGNER: Mandy McDonald Scallan
TYPEFACE: Minion Pro
PRINTER: McNaughton & Gunn, Inc.
BINDER: Acme Bookbinding

Library of Congress Cataloging-in-Publication Data

Smith, Dave, 1942–
  Hawks on wires : poems, 2005–2010 / Dave Smith.
    p. cm.
  ISBN 978-0-8071-4230-1 (cloth : alk. paper) — ISBN 978-0-8071-4231-8 (pbk. : alk. paper) —
  ISBN 978-0-8071-4232-5 (pdf) — ISBN 978-0-8071-4233-2 (epub) — ISBN 978-0-8071-4234-9
  (mobi)
  I. Title.
  PS3569.M5173H39 2011
  811'.54—dc22

                                                                                        2011016044

The author offers thanks to the editors of the following periodicals, in which the poems listed first
appeared, sometimes in different form: *Athelon:* "A Dream of a Bat"; *Birmingham Poetry Review:*
"Photograph of a Waterman, Bull Island, Virginia, Circa 1970"; *Blackbird:* "Allen Wheeler's Love
Tale," "Bourbon in a Cup," "Early Bird Dog Training," "Ruffed Grouse Feeding on Moonseed Berries,"
"Skating Waitress at the Circle Drive-In," "Woman, Snake, Percy Sledge"; *Cortland Review:* "A Gift
Boat"; *Fifth Wednesday Journal:* "Cumberland Reunion"; *Five Points:* "Blue Heron," "Bow Cleat," "The
Holy Mother of Connecticut Avenue," "Hooks," "Ode to Waffle House," and "Weekend Getaway";
Georgia Review: "Acetylene"; *Hopkins Review:* "Department E-7," "My Father's Tools," "Ron's Cat";
New Letters: "Christmas Concert, with Violin"; *New Yorker:* "Fireflies"; *Nightsun:* "Zydeco"; *North-
west Review:* "Fig Tree" and "Dissection"; *Poetry:* "Dry Cleaners"; *Potomac Review:* "Two Funerals
in the House"; *Sewanee Review:* "Rubber Men"; *Shenandoah:* "Tongue and Groove" and "Seventeen
Parts of a Duck"; *Southern Indiana Review:* "Colored Store," "Come-Along," "Goose Blind," and
"Moment of Here"; *Southern Quarterly:* "Fran's Barn"; *Southwest Review:* "Hawks on Wires" and
"Sawmill"; *Valparaiso Review:* "Glasses." "June Bug" was first published in *Something Understood:
Essays and Poetry for Helen Vendler,* ed. Stephen Burt and Nick Halpern (Charlottesville: University
of Virginia Press), 2009.

To Dee

and to my grandsons,
Baird Eley, Bowden Eley, Boyd Myrick, and Jed Smith

Contents

Contents

The Holy Mother of Connecticut Avenue

The Holy Mother of Connecticut Avenue

I.m. Larry Levis

Long ago we stole the white sheets from rope-lines in the South.
    Five from the University, in need
of a Halloween's prowl, seeking in the fall, full of seed,
    what even we didn't know, and came to the avenue of our country,
        its light golden. October heated us,

as if from graves we'd come. Strutting, I was nun-for-a-day,
    chest, cheeks magic markered, beer
waxed by dusk, and broke. So begged each face
    dragging the street, palmed coins, danced, and cried *The Holy Mother*
        of Connecticut Avenue loves you,

    and *Thanks, man.* Chanting folk songs, in chinos and Weejuns, we
        mugged *Make our people free!*
Oh selves, do you remember a black mother's *You!*
    one pint's greasy bucks she gave? Giggles, Christ's *Bless you, dearie,*
        her withering 100 proof kiss

    sears me still, boils in dreams, in doorway winks if I hear her
        say *What about those Selma girls?*
for I don't know a damn one and no snarl of Birmingham's dogs was
    anything I'd faced, not even my own sizzling
        of years I can't keep, so kneel

    now and try to know a tale of what good may be.

*

    If I had a hammer, we ghosts hollered, raised better but each
        joking, flipping up and back all any
countryman gave, and laughed as they did, Big Lyndon's house dead
    ahead, white as hope, and no bodies bagged yet,
        no Vietnam, no homeboys, just

3

us scooping each D.C. sweetie in high heels, silky bottom, or
        breasts we made *do wahs* to, God's
gifts, and we'd have to pay no matter what, so He said, who said Love
    thy neighbor. Well, right there she was, black
        skirt like skin, pink wool on top,

    two friends clicking in stride, and Daddios, it's *You!*
        In mold-stink, up stairs, bottles
rattled, we clamored on behind, down halls piss-soaked, in radio racket,
    slipping in vomit, by clang-wang-wang of pipes
        exploding like bombs, all

    windows just star-glass drifting on floors. We walked.
        Came on cockroach and hulls
of butts, cold pasta in bowls, lay down then on mattress, and I saw how
    our Monument's thick white rose shining,
        and rats' eyes flickered past

    unmoved by songs we kept humming, candles stubbed,
        Bud cans fetched from a room
wholly hung with fearful faces a child's hand had drawn. *Brother? You!*
    She said come, time's money. What child
        on small feet so faintly came?

    Did I even hear, or lift her head to say *Whose?* I was
        mostly drunk, the rustling hump
just what money was for, the sweet thing I was sliding inside a voice
    that kept saying *Do me, do it harder*—
        nothing more American.

                        *

    So many gone now, still the rancid joy lingers, what
        was in my head, we're singing
as if tall Mary Travers shimmers right there, no dragon we can't love,
    this is your land, my land, JFK's, Bobby's land,
        white boy blues, the jukebox

news poets were rhyming, pillows rank, sockets
　　　sputtering, death's lick-out
spooling from wires we don't see. Where someone snaps a light
　　black bubbles like a lingo I can't speak, now
　　　the wall's so hot if I pissed I'd

　　melt what hand held, then she screams, and I see
　　　the kid, flames flash up, eyes
are popping like corn, and I don't do a thing, no words will work,
　　just air my mouth gargles. Next falls that cold
　　　feathery rain, and Milton's angel

　　with me in flame-proof suit, that glassed, huffing
　　　savior you can't believe. He's fire
haloed, his black cheeks blow in, out, make a ball-squeezing bark
　　like a bullhorn's—MOTHER OF GOD,
　　　YOU'RE ON FIRE! Mostly

　　in life's roll-back of nights I can't sleep a fire-drake
　　　face comes down to me, lips making
"Jesus, Jesus"—me held, hair-hank and skin, shrieking, "You Son of Bitch
　　don't you know who I am? I'm the Holy Mother
　　　of Connecticut Avenue!"

　　　　　　　　　　　　　*

　　He whacked me, dumped me to wake in the street's
　　　dead dark. In culverts I darted,
in shade and filth, whatever worked, changing color, choking on words,
　　ghost in my terror. Going. As if he's my soul
　　　I hear that man one day scrape

　　chair, haze of barbecue thick, eyeing his guest, say
　　　"Pal, I got a good story for you."
Nobody's asked what's elbowed his mouth or why he whimpers or what
　　her name was or how it crisped his flameproof
　　　boots the color of her eyes,

for (his voice here crackles), "that cracker, buck naked,
     pale as Lulu's moonbeam run
off in DC's heart where I dumped him and can't one soul find him,
    say all I done said." Oh, he's years gone, and I call
     him up in a dream, he's talking

like salvation's bell tick-tocking, one fired-up mother.
    Is redemption just the irony
of a child torched, rooms of puke? *Please* feet on the street say. Days
    among the city's worst shade-slinkers I wandered,
     ate trash, stole from Goodwill

what fit me, snatched purse, spoke words numb
    as grunts, gray as stoned squirrels
standing to see me go, and no man knew me. Then one said *Holiness?*
    I froze as in his fist bounced quarters,
     a wonderful tinkly music

I knew would get me home. *You want home, you*
    gonna need what I give you.
Sun-glare like tin-foil in teeth. His fist upflicking bright coins.
    That grip closed like a mouth. *Dearie, who*
     you want to be? Can you beg?

*

All I knew I told fast, him crouched to hear, jabs
    he played like a fighter's who
told me all the wrong ways I went, once whipping off shades so I saw
    eyes opaled as smoke. *Blind,* I said. *Maybe,*
     but you's one I seen to save,

he sighed, breath old as a dumpster's bottom
    on that no-air boulevard,
heat sudden as August, my gut coiled, and then he says *We chose you!*
    Know why? Out-flung hand clawed and caught
     me, and I was free of answers,

nothing but gasps left. I watched His Grimness
        lift lips in dusk-glow. *Well,*
son, nobody knows everything, do they? He cackled and shook. *You*
        get your words right, any good they got
                come like a dog to you.

        Palms up, he begged for change, telling his tales
                at tear-wet faces I could not
face or fool, dopers and grannies, scum-thugs, whores saw: *You!*
        Time sparkled, water on streets as they gave,
                sniffing up, ladling it all out,

        him on haunches, touching, them darting on
                quick as the Zippo he flicked
if they laid a smoke on him. So why am I alone chosen to tell you
        what you know I don't know? *Ask the words,*
                they do the choosing, baby. . .

                                *

        You might say that old greaser of guilt was,
                if you saw him on a stoop,
only somebody's helpless Uncle Down-and-Out. And God knows
        that ought to make him gag and rise up, dear
                Saint Blind-as-the-Worms, way

        he made me do, head-hurts, eye-scabs painted,
                evil on me like the awfulest dirt
some choose to lie down in. I walked, I circled as he told me
        until I had it, life's most helpless look. Oh
                Love, they won't get past you,

        my Blind One whispered. *You all they got, Mother,*
                you make 'em sing, you bring 'em,
you don't stop! Stiff-legged, bent father and son we went on, him,
        me trolling words, taking tithes. He'd croon
                Empty 'em, son, scorch 'em

so they know they alive, fall like the leaves on 'em,
    talk 'til it's only dreams left. So
that's how one morning I woke in shades of ghosts. He said *You*
    taking over today. Oh, Unbelievers, I hear
        you saying it's only a poem

    for Christ's sake, where nothing happens, just lies,
        never the beautiful ends we dream.
But on I trooped, pitied, 'til a crone flung open a grin, cried *You!*
    Quarters clinked, she said *Tell us the tales*
        we got to pay for—I could

    feel hot dollars unroll like the Blind One's beard, now
        it seemed a song came smoking
where he stood—*like a baby crying.* I crossed myself. *Son, don't you*
    forget Birmingham, don't forget Selma, get up,
        tell all. I said how can I tell

    what I have not yet known? *Look hard, Son, you will*
        know when the bus stop. I begged
him to wait but he was fading, saying *Listen, we made you Holy*
    Mother of Connecticut Avenue to praise life.
        Ain't you alive? Don't you feel it?

    I heard voices as I boarded the bus, home a word
        I could pay for now. *Father, tell me,*
I whispered, *something more so I can't forget ever. Oh Holiness,*
    the ashen bus fumes said, *we gave you your tale.*

        Now go and tell it all.

Come-Along

The hook links to whatever's stable, plugged down, not to be budged
like my grandfather after the Depression, there's a pulley,
lines, ropes; wires useful for winching go around
the pulley circle's block, and they confuse the awful weight
of things that don't want to be moved, they shift tension,
they understand a lie, they go behind the implacable.
All you need then is the lever that ratchets through space,
linking the unimaginable place and the home thing that holds,
a man's will sufficient to imagine everything changed, and faith
there's no one bigger, stronger, or wielding a better machine against you.

Early Bird Dog Training

July day walking Finn number two, headstrong
pup who makes my arm twitch with fatigue, the pronged

stick I tap for stress hot incentive to him.
Ten months now, he hears every bird the same.

His heart boils, and soon his tongue lolls sidewise.
I don't know his limits, so leash his desire's

worst, though he bucks and huffs and whines. Heel, heel,
I bark, acolytes metering a suburb's field

until he's caught by a goldfinch. Is this it?—wild
canary, butterfly yellow, that flits, scolds,

seaming the beaten path with beauty's signal.
How bold, notes from a hidden branch that trembles!

Yet I can't find the nesting tree, nor can dog,
who, unmoved by form, points not song but log.

Dissection

I found an essay in the reading room of Jiffy Lube, a memoir,
a medical student walking us through the steps. It meant
discovery as old oil was getting flushed, pages readers
soiled and tore like personal history. Gaps required a leaping
mind, maybe the kind the body had, I thought. No news
of what sex started things, its failed poetry, if different
parts decoded fear or pride, or football's broken shoulder
and chronic ankles, not even the rheumatoid arthritis
that bends a lady's knuckles like those hooked ones resting
quiet beside me. I thought how I loved a woman's
long, slender fingers, and remembered the blunt, fat
stubs my daddy wrapped around screwdrivers. Go get me one,

he'd scream, whatever it was one of, and I wouldn't see which
screw, bolt, washer meant something, so I tried to keep
the hole in mind, if there was one, and looked in the usual
drawers like he told me to, pushing aside this or that wrapper
laid over spark wires, plugs, torn envelopes, and dug into
stashed car mags, rods rehabbed, welding tips, tech talk,
chrome's care lingo, paint layered like desire, then way
deeper than imagined, still hoping only to find what I was
sent to bear back, I saw the hand, the body coiled, naked, sun
running on it like gasoline. I could feel her suddenness,
like match or spark. Stunned, I stayed long, the long scream
the least of what I would remember, and keep, still, like prose.

June Bug

Scarabaeidae

The carapace—is that it?—shrugging forward
like a Roman war-wagon, dark gleam
from the sloped shoulders and the lowered head,
itself helmeted, swaying from side to side,
as if the great weight, with one slip
of purchase, might haul everything backward,
the massive thighs and horn-embraced
legs that dig ponderously, the tip-toe
forenails that grip surface, least or best,
and those already wounded, so they seem,
trailing appendages, brogans dragging.
To this, under the fore-armpits
I tie my string, sun like an egg's center, and wait.
No sound. At first, no movement. Wait.
Then the big head, slippage until some
crack in the earth appears, and slant rays
of light leveraging it forward, grass blades
bent, twigs gone over like bodies,
small combatants scurrying aside, now and then
a pause, the heavy hold on air I think
is death until, at last, it rises up.
Shrugs on. Soon it will be dusk, dinner.
The earth is darker, a coolness floats.
Already the story breathes me. So I wait
as the string plays into darkness until all is
tug and touch, imagined, the big thing breaking off.

Bow Cleat

In the midst of a field, I saw it again.
Like a hood ornament,
the long v-slope like a forehead,
like two horns flashing the sun's high torment.

So I thought of the surf patting in
that day long ago, a boy
dawdling the rabbity marsh line,
the ragged drifty patch of oil-soaked plyboard.

A bright and well-imagined grip to strike
a knot to, holding on.
And walked all that inlapping afternoon
remembering, as if nothing would ever go loose.

Rubber Men

You may say they exist only in stories, but I saw them.
My grandmother, wide as a washing machine, paid
twenty-five cents and we boarded the Phoebus bus,
me trailing, she like a woman summoned to the gods.
By low, squat houses, in hot cottons, we rode until
we flew past all we knew. I knew her stories would
begin when her big sweaty chest heaved, so I watched.

We had our snacks in brown bags, munching as she told
one about a troupe of catchers, tall women, and rope
swingers, and rubber men rolling in knots, and caged
by walls of eye-balling boys and girls there would be fire
swallowers, sword eaters, the world's weirdest of all
people. Who were, she said, exactly like me. I wanted
to know where they came from. You'll see, she said, wait.

The tent wasn't a tent at all but high-domed, with stars
of lights hung in silvery upside-down bowls, and hot
with us bleachered and wedged in. I waited for the romp
elephants might make in sawdust, for gurgling lions.
A few seedy clowns leaned about where ropes dangled,
as if like monkeys they'd decide suddenly up or down.
Thinking was what she said they were doing. You can't

see that happen. I waited. Then a brown tiny car came
sputtering through its own oily cloud, coughed to a stop,
so its driver spilled out his window, lanky and slinky,
wearing his black pajamas. I laughed. Then another,
another, maybe a dozen unfolded forth, each angled so
if he'd turned he'd be lost like fallen stars. I thought
where they live they must eat nothing like fried chicken,

my grandmother's gold in our bags, or potatoes creamed,
or hammy summer beans I loved, cornbread's butter
oozing as easy as the men had from that car. How many
were they, the shadows? Surely all dead now, smiles of
grease passing like joy over us kids, bored clowns yawning,
who couldn't or wouldn't speak as if punished, or lonely.
Why have I never stopped dreaming what it felt like to be

one of the shadows packed so tight you'd laugh but think
he can't get out. Then one would. I was too high to see
eyes lift up like a dog over a still-warm plate, or know
how a face slowly opened up to the fill-in of our gasps
if one punched another, or tumbled to rain-like applause,
the tricks just stopped as, disciplined, they climbed down,
unbelievably, into a car sputtering off, us left waiting in light.

Colored Store

He'd have Nehi Grape, Pepsi was mine,
and peanuts, with salt extra I'd fetch.
A can by the shack door. But

sometimes pickled pig's foot, our white
teeth, pink gums shining, and him
way tickled by boys he'd sell

anything to, even a hot can of beer late
Saturday night. What was it he had
we wanted? The truck, our big ride,

rolled up to his whistle, dust skinned all,
radio's late innings, long fingers
at chin, "Whatchall want?" White

boy I last saw laid in the dead sheet,
skin yellow as bird-beak, squealed
like an owner, who had grinned

already ass-first on that counter. "Ain't
nothing you got," said white hand in jar
where pink feet slowly bobbed.

So I'd say it, too, trying to learn how
words manage men, and meant
I'd have an answer one day.

He'd stick paw in and swoop out a fist
wiggle of pink little dancers, big
smile all we paid, and me

hot mornings in the South, fifties, sixties—
salted nuts like blisters on my tongue.
Drank Pepsi, said nothing at all.

Sawmill

When I come here it is in dawnchill and the sweet gold mound
of wood chips holds still, not growing. I wear the thin-soled
hunting boots L. L. Bean sells, blue work shirt,
jeans raveling end to end. I take notes
among the toe-scuffing of the old ones who, before me,
boys, waited here, smoking, talking of women they'd touch

in low whispers, then all week they rise, work, and walk out
the clay road with the odor of wood on them.
I like this wait in the glittery first light
under the pine shawl that keeps them,
faces vague in blown tobacco and coffee steam,
each Monday kicking at dust until the time comes around,

the little lies each repeats like the spit-and-whine of the saw-start.
A mockingbird's throat-tearing notes remind me
of pulleys that ripple in sunbursts, of dew,
and the glaze of oiled gears, and flashes
turning the day on like a woman's thigh glimpsed
at the corner café. Then sleek planks hauled out steadily,

the heartwood unbending and soft all at once, its ghost-limbs
with aureoles drawing down calloused hands, the far
bang of the stacks ubiquitous as the soul
with its blinked-off hurting, sweat in the eyes,
and the shadowless striding of noon when a man looks up
to say *Already?* . . . and the name nobody speaks, spoken, cry

at the wheel, hers, that was wailing always, always, and she who
came back each time it would slam off, each man's
face then looking as if it were planed
from the loud silence. I like to smell the mint here
in the hurt hours of morning when I think of the men,
whose heads would turn to follow a siren miles off, necks

stiffened with family blood, who told me it was no matter,
and laughed when a woman said *She's kissed another,*
a voice in windows, screened nearly from sight.
I come here at the last dark and the women
in many low houses watch me, their rising habitual,
their breath still blowing fire into old sticks, coiling smoke

above each roof drifting away like time-swallowed words.
Soon enough stars fading and pale as sliced pine.
I like to see the light come up, the snake's
dawdle in sawdust, and the wheel freckled
like a girl's face, abandoned until
Monday, that women called the cock-cutter, grinning.

Acetylene

Cigarette's spit of white, fire-tip's red-orange of Christmas on the hearth,
fierce blue, yellows, more you'd go blind if you looked at it, so I looked
where black gloves hooded him to the elbow, the angled sizzle
and metal-forming force of hands that did the work of the imagined
lodged there somehow, palpable as souring after-pour of his breath,
his body slumped, the weld unshatterable as his truth at the dinner table.
That black of the world pure, then things walking forth out of it,
the hiss and whistle of the gas, my grandfather singing them from memory.

Fig Tree

Maybe it's grown back, enigma, blossomer,
    shrouding the fence I helped them build,
        as a boy does, watching, asking all but

unanswerable questions, its age like mine,
    visible in the limbs, thickened flesh, nicked
        body no one hears groaning its statement,

its broken smell of green buds all at once
    all opened, the way the mind can be, too,
        when a song strikes, or a book goes flat,

or a girl's legs, that hissing of skin,
    make a heartbreaking sign if she moves.
        My future's revealed. I know the force

that longed to see it fall, damp spring's
    rot, but why split its flesh willingly,
        its skins lie, each little torso raw, pink,

alive to merciless sun that blisters? I saw
    my grandmother's thinned hair, the black
        roots as she bent, lifting the unwanted.

Staves, teeth like a rat's, ran in rows
    where I banged my stick to knock away
        fruit's white, drying, eternal message.

Skating Waitress at the Circle Drive-In

We're grandparents now. Then bright steel fins lined up, all
the fathers waiting to die in wing chairs at home. The beat
oozed from open car window to car window, each bearing
a tray the waitress tilts and locks. Then a hand slides out
dropping change as she twirls, who's also dead, her flying
ponytail electric, and just then the pink Cadillac, and the black

faces as glass smoothes slowly down, smoke hazing inside.
That's all it takes. I can hear knuckles crack, the words
like flecks of spit in summer air, like looping bats visible
in high moth-swirls of light. But nothing happened the way
everybody thinks. Milkshakes gone, we slumped, unbuckled,
cruised the river's salt marsh, boats fishing where it's lonelier

than we knew, some asleep on deck, maybe learning how
beautiful shore lights are. Soon a girl slips off a pink sweater
where we've pulled in to park. We don't expect headlights,
so many cars, guys piling out for the fight, one bleeding
on the warm Oldsmobile. Tomorrow I'll wax my dad's Ford,
drag the old mower over wasps, shoot baskets with anybody

at school, trying hard not to see the black face all pushed out
for what's coming, the skater saying *We don't serve niggers.*
Whoosh, hot air leaves my mouth, ball drops, I see him,
teeth bright as a bug light. A black back seat face whines
We don't eat them either so night breaks like ice thrown
on pavement, like a ball slapped. I felt each humped tar strip,

every small body struck turned to goo I'd never get off.
If I tell you I'm watching TV's b-ball, I'm watching him
watch me watching the dark, a man surely alive as I am.
Who never was stabbed, or struck, or rose up to say
Fuck you to that ass skating away, to her pimply cheeks
sucking in, out, to the gum-chew, rat-hair the sailors cried for.

Who didn't have a reason to whistle any word we might hear.
Then lips, nipples, the usual sounds poured at the dark, also
fists and feet rustle, and ticking in the head. Why, as if floating,
did our bodies bang out of control? Who brought us that baby
in the back seat? Nights skating until the Circle closed.
How aimless all was, like sperm puffed up, beating a way home.

Allen Wheeler's Love Tale

The night he saw his old man on top,
Allen Wheeler said, he nearly shit
with fear, but not because of what
he saw, which wasn't much, it
was he wasn't supposed to be where
he was, and he was, and he thought
Hell, I'll catch his worst strap sure,
and to hear him tell it, now almost
crying, he struck first, shouting. Dad
up and grabbed his belt and wailed.

I've thought this over and think now
that Allen Wheeler lied, as boys do
when first faced with crude facts
involving their mother and more.
I can't say what he saw exactly, or
what fear he felt, but it isn't only
place or time, wrong as may be, that
sets a father's scream ringing clear.
One day our son came in and knew
to choose the door we couldn't shut.

It's like so much else, said my dearest,
just ignore what hurts, as you don't
see the heart attack on the street, pass
the man slugging his child, wish a girl
luck with a flat on a fast, dark road.
And if you stop, trouble has its sly way
of sticking long after you have gone.
Just wave, think what Allen Wheeler
said that no dad can bear, keep on,
think how the story will be told,
years later, at the table, finally alone.

Croaker Bucket

A bucket of fish appears, silver croakers, others black spot
behind gill, sun-glint on slime and skin.

Then hands—blood-spotted, stained by engine's bleed?—follow.
Scales clinging to hair, Masonic ring, gold face

floating up, mouth stretched, a weird grin as if hooked, wide
eyes startled by me, because I, a boy, have leaned

from the pier to see what a croaker is. Overhead jet fighters
from Langley AFB drown the faint croak,

and gull-anger and the words dying as his lips gulp, and silence.
Then I see the other one, sitting, leaning at

upright tiller-stick, hands slack at hull behind, blood-and-scale
smeared, and the first man bobs, white-whiskered,

as incomers and outgoers pass in the water's rough-up of slips,
and though I try to keep my eyes on fish

I see the face has come and sits on my plank and is crying
"Daddy"—it croaks, too, like the bucket,

something I am never going to understand—but is that what I am
trying to tell? The first man watched the other,

faced the traffic of boats, unrolled his knee-high waders, rolled
them back on like a too-big skin, making scales

fall and go dry in sun-flare, the smell starting that I already knew,
the way I knew under the water everything is

huge in its secret life, electric, ticking, the dim shadow that fills
the bucket with chartreuse stiffs, each

convulsing last flesh-thrust opening the gill-gasp on the purple
beauty even this far away I see him watching.

Bourbon in a Cup

Today, alone, I feel the ease of sinking in a dream.
Boathouse ivy hung in your hair, roping us close,
as I settled with you, love, in wet grass, slick
and cold like the top of the Hatteras yacht where,
trespassers in stars once, we had been diving,
then making love, and then came night crawl
of lights with friends, that house party, a marsh
by Back River, traffic along Victory Boulevard.
Voices on the patio doubted our future forty
years ago, near the Air Force base. Now-dead,
their babies unborn, or asleep, married, joking.
Steaks sizzled on the cooker, sweat on beer cans.
My cup, lit like a small universe, kept pulsing.
Be still, you said, your dress rolled, yellow wasps
like tiny angels hanging on it. You grinned, held
your breath, waiting. I felt you alive at my shirt.

If we are dead now, walking naked in Heaven,
where our friends stand to tease and whoop at us,
I'll say our marks are the bites of those insects
we learned to carry, not recoiling, but enduring.
Say nothing of the nights we did not touch, hours
we abandoned love. I smell mowed-over onions
in that grass, the sweat mixed with swamp-salt,
colognes, cigarettes, meat charring, flood tide.
If they ask what we did by the boats, we'll say
we smoked, we swam among them, we ran away
and married—we signed, we paid, we were alive.
In my dream you enclosed me again, old words
fumed between us like mists of gnats, the unseen
not digging at my skin, not biting, but wanting in.
They will know us as we are, you said. Yes, weeds
in our mouths, ivy where hair was, the taste in that cup.

Department E-7

Department E-7

on the door: Dept. E-7
—"Why God Permits Evil," Miller Williams

The West Baltimore father who confessed to throwing
his 3-year-old son off the Key bridge told police that
demons made him do it.
—*Baltimore Sun*

1.

A man, mocha-skinned, black hair, pig-tailed,
   holds the pay telephone
      in one hand,

bangs it against the silver upright casket
   of glass until
      all of it shakes so hard

I think it will topple, or the panes will explode,
   but nothing happens, and then
      he screams

into the little black holes, throws up
   flecks of spit,
      flesh stains on walls

visibly scarred as if by fingernails, magic
   marker's graffitied names.
      His breath fumes, scarf

tied at brow, like horns, and we waiting
   for change
      in the convenience store

can hardly believe
   this hurricane in a box, wreckage
      of soul that now kicks

what walls him in, hurled side to side,
        pain-scalded, demons
                tearing his camo-jacket.

2.

"Omigod, what in hell," says
        a woman, young, soiled,
                bleached-out waitress

uniform, her just-bought
        Marlboro light not yet lit
                falling, "Omigod," so

I think of my daughter at the mall, sorrow
        and love, her cell phone losing
                the link and boyfriend,

repeating, in fear, "Omigod, Omigod"
        as real as dinner where we
                sit, wife, me

hearing the high, thin yoke of prayer,
        a mantra, I think, that weird
                numbness I once used

to chant, blue suit of the Air Force
        on me, dropping my son
                at day care, Nixon hurling

us at Laos, Cambodia, radio
        manic, the Stones drowning
                our cries, my son's

winging   tiny arms.

3.

"Might be drugs," clerk
        slurs, Budweiser shoved

in bag a boy's body-size. Then
        we see the kid, legs kick, mouth
                gasps, and, Jesus,

he's pale, naked, cow-brown
        eyes, freezing, diaper
                ripped, I can't help

wanting the hate I feel, suddenly
        loving the kid, knife of
                mania in my heart, but

the man steps out, squeezes
        the body that wails—same
                face, smaller—then he grins,

shuts bi-fold doors, strides calm
        to car, powers up, straps
                down the kid, wiggles

himself deep, locks in, like a pilot
        forehead pinched, turns
                into the wind-swirls,

shifts, rolls, darts past buckling
        air-wakes of trucks, is gone,
                shrunk like a toy floating off.

4.

It's afternoon, school not out,
        yellow buses lumber,
                seagulls fall, hungry, flakes

at black trees, lifting whatever
        road-kill, mashed, is
                visible. Today ice,

forecast, makes iron day
        last, taste bitter, of ash
                of grit ascending in splash

from berms, gray bridge
        abutments tide-marked,
                world-slime, us gazing

up road, dreaming
        ways out of plant lots,
                butter sun, sweet lying

with a woman, beach breeze,
        handful of families
                on sand, some buried

like me in traffic dying. How shall
        we escape what's breaking
                ahead, heave it from us?

5.

Climbing the Key Bridge I slow
        over mud, marsh, boats
                half-sunk, duck blinds

like prayer stalls unused, glare
        of taillights, traffic's steam,
                creatures jammed up,

then stop on a metal grid.
        Each eye flicks, inches
                forward, dented green Toyota

dead right, emergency flashers
        like anger. I see him, I think,
                coat-bloated. Or I'm

scared, caught, guessing. Face
        an instant's all he is,
                less, and I'm over

the crest, wind eddies so strong
        bridge, car, bodies fuse, easy
                to believe a plummet's

coming, now's exposed
        crack ticking, us just
                blood something's

jiggled. Could I have stopped him, son
        of a bitch at the edge? You're
                too late, seagulls shriek.

Black chops below, horns
        honk as if God wants me
                to move on, so I do,

queasy and tracked in mid-air.
        Drive, the grid snicks at
                each of our tires, rust welds

and rivets cradling us
        over the deep we wheel
                past, trembling.

6.

Which word can say what
        a man faces? Phosphorous
                bursts blow away demons

and Skywalker grins, righteous,
        weightless horrors drift
                to dust, bottoms

of film cans, only dust,
        no bodies in framed light.
                Death piled in every shade

we touch and breathe.
        We snap on TV news, woman
                crying "he ain't done it!"

"He love us," she pleads, but
        big smile suddenly zig-zagged
                to mouth-hole, tongue that

explodes, "He call I say go to hell,
        bring my goddamned baby
                home!"

The terrified, breathless out-gust
        a small mouth has, it must
                be joy the baby feels spun

skyward, his daddy's tossed
        him up to fly, oh, forever
                he waits to be caught,

like my daughter, fingers
        crossed in our kitchen, squealing
                "Omigod, Omigod," boyfriend

floating in darkness,
        cell-phone fishing her close,
                love's barbed words

faint, trolling, hidden
        from all, even the standing-there
                one, car-stopped at bridge-yawn,

flag-draped freighter slipping out,
        faces gazing up, his gazing down,
                sea-hawk's clutch agape at

whatever falls. Wing-plunge and blood
        spurt. Up here it's only wreckage,
                look hard or don't, eye-blink,

and last glint swirling, tumbling,
        water that seems all there is.
                Except scream. Except splash.

Moment of Here

No one gives a boy permission to come, you
pass under law, what happens is dreamed,
forgetting you are alive, and you enter as

I do, slightly clothed, almost criminal,
because no one imagines you fishing, or sees
.chokecherry, poison ivy, Queen Anne's lace

drop itself, move aside, or shuddery crown
of orange bugles, Virginia creeper, fall
soft as fingertip touch of milkpod, and burr

that clings like a family's reputation. I
pass copperhead-quick on the path, stirring
one blue jay from her nest, then settle

with quiet, moves any monarch displays, ease
shirt off my gold-tanned skin, and feel a tent
of pink mimosa lower itself on me

as if a god ordered guard for whatever
heart beats this bank. I unspool a spider line
hooked to my pole, its bamboo trembling,

the creatures I have tied in my room's
midnight beginning now to flutter like one
or two delicious words, and cast, gulp

of breath, back-flip of wrist keeping me free
of wisteria so thick some lighters take it
for the world. Small fish rise, try me, then

bigger ones from a mantle of seed-green,
orbiting, bluer shades fixed ahead of me.
I crouch as if praying to turn a mouth

open before time was, or law, or owners.
Line ticked out, I start to cast for all I know
watches, believing I am, it is, ready.

My Father's Tools

T-squares, draftsman's table-world, rotatable, kept
draped in oil-cloth, secrets of pencils to be pointed
like long guns, scrolled blue-prints I believed full
of treasure, not keel, magazine, bulkhead, or deck
where scattered the exploded carrier's thousands of legs.

*

His dithering, redundant language was never answerable
to me, numbers, that solve-for-X slide rule's tongue
slow as courage when I needed it, digits of obedience
I couldn't get right, like a man with an idea standing
on a bridge rail, cold swoon of current his signal to come.

*

When he died I got his gizmos. They're gone now, cases,
too, and velvet socks, some big as shovels, or piked
circle-makers. I liked the brass-edged T, axe-wicked
if swung in play, for which two or three times
blood shone on a friend. I lay to be whipped by his hand.

*

I have moved often, scattered them, boxes burst. Things
hooked to things, broke. Bad smell, off-eye of level,
useless beauties. He wouldn't believe how cheap
calculation is, cell phones, computers, bombs.
What would he say to me in a letter—caught, no answers?

*

His hand printed everything, his lines held up space,
his trust in blueprints, jointed, unyielding. I learned
stress, this against that, and feel for the edge.
I had his Masonic apron, shotgun by J.C. Higgins,
class ring, the MIT certificate, engineer of warships.

*

Why did he not tell me water bleeds, nothing's worse, seeps,
damps, leaks, drips, rots, runs, rust, holes, bottoms
no legend reveals? Who has seen his tools,
pitted by now, dirt-scabbed, hung like chickens
at flea markets, broken by all they know? Reward offered.

A Gift Boat

Mary Alice—was that her name?—my student, pink hair, a poet,
quoter of Coleridge, brought me to the strange craft
a wild storm, fizzling out, left in the marsh. She shrugged,
few rules out there. "You want it," she said, "it's yours."

A jet fighter's wing-tip fuel pod from the fifties. Silver hull
somebody'd halved, pine seat, bamboo mast, tube outrigger,
a tarp for sail, so light she whizzed like a dragonfly. But
no keel to steer, stick tiller, just the feel of moving to know

how to tack for wind, shooting away, losing all, working again.
You'd call me to supper, voice skating on that blue. I'd tiller
to shallows, throw my body over waist-deep, try to set up
angles wind might grip, what the fathers taught. You watched.

Soon I was circling, sliding, singing to trees, untranslated clouds,
gulls. Going deeper, I wasn't afraid I'd be becalmed or caught
by currents turning strong. Light, air, water worked with me
to make ideas, hours fly. Day after day this scooter showed

how to lean on tide and shadow and touch. I could not go fast
enough, far enough for its secrets. Then it was gone, random
storm, a night piling up driftwood, flood-slosh, as if new
rules dragged all away. I woke to a blown sparrow's corpse

afloat at the tie-post, like a poem no effort could keep alive.
How could I know in such love what is worthless? Eyes closed,
we swayed in moonlight, you, me, that no-cost skidder going
where we didn't know we could go, or zigzagging like sentences,

dizzied by wakes of schooled cruisers. Alone, then, you waited,
my hand waving for joy or despair, barely in sight, and all
you could see. A canoe like that—how could it last?—you said.
Gift of the little muse, whooshing circles, tangents, like words.

Ruffed Grouse Feeding
on Moonseed Berries

Three of them, one watching us, wise head turned
so its eye, a wet black moon, fills. The spring
of its body, half hidden, drums bare ground
behind a fallen leaf. But two—fanned wings,

leaning close like Romeo and Juliet about
the other, whose talon has ripped the turf—
levitate. Their necks, breasts stretch up and out,
beaks, in hunger, part, and in the abrupt

white sky that must be summer's longest hour
blue moonseed hangs luscious, gravid, lewd
almost, the magnetic, shivering glamour
of these songless ones, feathers like truths

no one but sweet dreamers attend, a riff
of joy never snatched by the unseen hawk,
or gobbled by rat, or toppled, stiffed
by the thick-bellied rattler coiled upon rock.

Audubon's plate 41, American triad,
two redeemed, nearly, one left, and empty
heaven, untouched paper, moon's acid,
blistering glow waiting on all that will breed.

Blue Heron

For Betty Adcock

Neck like a coat hanger unbent, abandoned
almost, the look of a closet,
patches of cloth, paper, dust, the last
steps imagined, gone,

no ripple where she stands, gray or blue
depending on the slant sun, one
of the invisibles, as a friend
calls the women poets of

the South. Lake flat as paper, the day's end
electric at her feet, steel nerve unturned,
turning, eye wide, she prefers
to hold her ground

alone, six-foot wings, the swift flicking
her mouth is a small, silent lightning.

Woman, Snake, Percy Sledge

I heard this woman calling as if out of my memory,
or a dream, it was summer, doors and windows open.
When I went outside into the heat I felt the coiled
overwhelming press of despair because she screamed,
a voice hanging in that sultriness because no one
was answering, panic was setting in. I don't say
she wasn't thinking when she groped the rose legs,
trying to reach past dangerous thorns, her wish
to remove weeds, vines, to open a space for beauty,
but neither glove nor balm nor any protection had her.
What of poison ivy. . . why would she not ask?. . . or red
diamonded spider, even the sun itself more corrosive
than the dullness of staying safe? Still, if it's a garden
you want, you can hardly avoid the occasional lift
of a head, quick and coppery in shade, a bare touch
of fingertips will do, no one seeing the saint's lick of
consequence that quickens. That's what she had, who
was bouncing her body in petunias and hydrangeas
up and down, like a joke in mint and shafting sunlight,
bumping backward so the startled-over wheelbarrow
threw up its rake, its tangled Virginia creeper, its roots
of god-knows-what, festering and knotting so many
years, her hands shoved up in surrender, then falling
as she fell, without plan or luck, as if her flesh had
nothing to do with what it was doing, she was way
beyond fear, and a model mother, but kids long out
of mind and, really, isn't this how it happens? I was
outside the fence, then leaping over to her, shovel
scooping up dark, chopping the head off, brain
blank as a spaniel. Then it was done. What I remember
ought to be the finch-dart of her brown eyes, the blind
glaze, the leaf-limp thirst that can come to all things,
the hiding grotto where house and ground meet
like a man and woman, naked, surprised. Mostly

the words she was wailing got me, like Percy Sledge
opening another supermarket with *When* (or *If?*) *a
Man Loves a Woman,* that irrational love we love
selling Baton Rouge Fords. With her now in my arms,
it looked like we were waltzing, her heavy as mulch,
me touching her forehead, her hot lips, then sucking
the bitten hand. Soon I felt myself swelling with her
breasts that fumbled to escape her delightful little
frock all green stained. I cooed, "please settle down,"
I said, "have you called your husband," and all the time
I was thinking of the cool gaze that had lain waiting.
It was always right there, listening, watching us.
It didn't want to bite, it hadn't thought of it, easy
wake-up, day unpredictable, but one touch changes
everything, fate doesn't want to be commanded.
I could see I'd strike, too. Now I hoped for a siren,
my mind raced with things I might do, home projects,
Internet searches, names, letters unwritten, the coiled
body of a young woman I had loved years ago, saying
goodbye. My neighbor was dangerously heavy now.
It wasn't noon yet and I couldn't leave her alone.
"Please," she said, her breath licking out, like despair.
Unspeakable, my heart. The only answer was call 911,
find another woman who'd handle my emergency,
bright voice asking who the victim is, who you are.
I felt my neighbor panting as if sexually exhausted.
I'd speak very calmly, I told myself, I'd remember
to survey the yard, green ways in, out, obstructions,
false steps. I'd move deliberately, confess the woman
is not dead yet in my embrace, but very weak, and, no,
the snake's alive, though already forgotten, moved on.
The woman on the telephone would say *hold on, please.*

Fran's Barn

Marshfield, Vermont

1.

A great wooden box full of what she calls his toys,
the time-quieted Saab, hunched, neighbor's gift,
relic of a tractor, Ford, clean, bony, ready
when snow ends, when green tips appear,
two dark-hulled survivors, convertible, coupe,
tarped to wait like parents in dust-moted foyer
where some story, stilled now, is underway
night after day after night. The lightless ease is
welcome, pastoral like a ship's inside, odd bits
of sound he likes to stand in, feeling beams
unknown old ones laid against time, this, then
what's coming, cradled hours, the wood whining.

2.

Behind this the Jug brook goes on trying to talk,
birch shifts hour by hour as if to hear better, trembling
apple's blood-red nubs a child's heart-pulse, maybe
ornaments hung for holiday, forgotten, to chime
again in ice rimes that will hold a rose bud, its pink
show starting soon like hope. Wood smoke has the air
like a grandmother's perfume on a sidewalk, he
almost knows who it was, there's a little longing.
But what stops him is the plow, black point
jamming the plank-strapped door open, still ready
enough to split the earth for its meaning. Rigid,
his dad stood here on the visits. A man's place.

3.

He feels the stitches strain, his skin heaving up, out.
She's watching from the kitchen window, but
what could she do if he toppled as if shot?

What could she do if he would lie there smelling
onions just cut by the drive? Help's all so far away
from these acres he mows, pushing, breath the sump's
gargle into the brook. Tomorrow they'll fly, clinic,
Houston, no stacked books, framed children, cry
of ravens the color her hair used to be, new words
like instruments chilled, calibrated. In the barn
he tries to imagine them but all that comes is how
the door opens, the darkness flutters, day blinks blue.

4.

It's interesting, isn't it, he'd like to say to someone
not there, things in this dark look kept, saved up,
a person's whole life translated. But nothing
leaves, it's protected, and rotting too, what comes
in does that. He shoves the plow aside, face
flecked with a cut weed, then gazes in a moment.
People ask him what it's all for. It's for itself's
the best answer he's summoned, the Citroën
floating weirdly up, down because it can,
same barn swallows nesting their old corners,
because they can, his barn kept because he can
love it all and he can shut the doors again tonight.

Seventeen Parts of a Duck

In 1969, enlisted to go to war, I lucked in, stateside, nights teaching
men to write, days paying
death benefits to weepy faces, then got out, burned uniforms,
forgot it all. Except
my last class, old men like me now.

One week to prepare for going back "into the world." I said
Men, today write a definition of something.
Words came broken, naked as bodies in Langley's Base Hospital,
3B, where we met.
I still see the medic doubling me up

with laughs at his thesis: "A duck with seventeen parts
will live and function good as a duck." My height and weight
but old as old wars, snake-quiet,
just back from Vietnam,
he hinted things he couldn't say

except in mysteries, in supply lists of parts, eye, upper and lower
scapula, legs,
knee, foot, asshole (technically not a part, I joked), spine,
feather, rib, beak,
liver, covert, gut (guts? I red-lined), and heart.

So what? I scrawled at bottom line, pushing him past bare facts
to claim a greater thing. He tried.
"Bible says girl ducks have no rib." "Assholes is always
blown up first." "Scapulas are
like angels' wings. With pulleys." No

logic made me howl like his. He revised, cut or added parts, each
funnier, tied up as he'd cupped, wrapped
the stitched thing, a dick, arm, half a brain he'd pack
home to start again.
His giggle showed no

fear or pain, scheme or purpose. *Why this?* I wrote. *Why that?*
Was his thesis a catechism: "If each
of the seventeen parts of any duck is present
and in working order, unit will function as a duck"?
On the sixth day, reading aloud,

standing, as we hid faces in a moonwhite room, eyes darting
like a man in a ditch, he
transformed it all in a storm of mangled Latin parts,
seventeen, his definition
as solid as Genesis, then began to hum

his gospel truth. "If we the people treat the duck equal, America,
it can live and grow to be
a duck." Our breath escaped like a body bag that hissed, but
onward he read, no end in sight,
as if no way

the world could stop words he'd formed up to fight, a leader
of quacking things: "Good duck
stands on two feet." "Spineless duck spoils a flock."
"Dress uniform," my notes said,
"Lifer." I meant enemy.

Older, I remember his medals, starred and saintly, hung colorful
as parts that might, if he lived enough,
someday make sense beyond theories and lists, even
a tale I'd never got the joke of.
Oh, Groucho,

this was duck soup, not an idea on the horizon, just words.
Six days I watched him work
to gouge one sentence, then another. Head tilting
side to side as if to see
what a poet looks for, his wet lips mimed my *So what?*

I was getting out soon myself. What was a list to me?
When Saigon fell, from choppers
people dropping like tomatoes, Nixon's comrades, we jibed,
he spit, "Screw you, kiddies,"
folded his notebook, and waddled out

of my life. It wasn't much. I kept on writing. I didn't ask
where he'd go on that seventh day—who
must be, like me, somewhere in the world yet.
Does he stand a man
a drink, a joke about fowl?

I like to think of my brothers laughing as our hero quacked
his packing order, those days
we lived to go, ducks unfixed, senseless as war. Seventeen
holy parts. Why?
That's what I'll ask, if ever we meet again.

Jury Duty

Room-door squints open, like eye of a needle, then faces,
tables numbered, nails pecking laptops neoned,
games, ear-cords, boogaloo, Mozart, maybe
jazz. We all wait to be chosen, news no one wants.

A child cries down the hall, hard, then softer, then deep sobs.
Pages turn for those already given up to histories, tales,
sex, murder, the gods, mysteries one man
taps his foot to reading young Keats in Baltimore.

The fatherly hum of a Coke machine lulls the windowless
room like a nursery, yawns of innocence breaking out.
In the principal's office, accused, I tried
faint answers, getting stiff, wordless with my fear.

We will see the offender tremble. Together we will hide
in the fields of our imagination, holding still,
like any creature denying himself, head down
in long quiet confined, in halls and numbered rooms.

Tense, not speaking, we listen. Here and there one rises up
and goes. We count, jaws clenched, those with us.
Sundays our childhood streets were the same.
If a moving figure—what's he up to?—we chose sides.

It grew dark, we ate, we read from animal books, fell asleep
loving the brave ones. That's when we were deceived.
Tomorrow one of us would be grown, hooves
galloping off. Some, dreaming, alone, sank inside.

Now in a corner the little plea of coins, the heavy thump,
feet scraping, muffled words like truth and beauty
the same, never enough. They slip from the side
of the mouth, of the tongue with its precious wisdom.

Weekend Getaway

Noisy, sullen traffic plows past the docks, leaving the wake
full of croakers, eels, blowfish you can't get rid of, bait, hooks

swallowed hard. In bed with me, you rise, walk to the window.
It slices you in half light, your fecund smell sudden as exposed

river plants. You weep, too young, as a small propeller blades
the bottom of thought with guttural language I once understood.

Wind-shifts are deviling surface and horizon. In Li Po's poems
a black river capriciously flows, leaving pearl mist on the arm

a girl has bared. Night barges its inevitable cargo to black.
The shirtless boy sleeping in the bow that bobs comes awake.

In the same boat, a man like me casts his old lure and it sinks
with muffled cry. When you piss, the splash is a vase breaking.

Up and down the river groans gather like thunder. Betrothed,
in hulls bent men ride it out, crabs clenched, whipped by froth.

Ron's Cat

Mice in my wall remind me of a cat long dead
Ron loved to stroke, anonymous on the bed
as it was at the door that night of blowing rain.
Dried, fed, claiming the fire, he needed no name.

What he needs is a bell, Ron said, trees twittering
with robins, finches, then a cardinal's string
of feathers on porch steps, nothing Ron could change.
He hung the brass bell with body's fearful shake.

Claws dug blood from a black and white neck.
He'll accept things, Ron said, two, three weeks.
Today a dog, where I walked, leaped before a car,
its broken leash trailed, brakes breaking the stare

I'd fallen to—starting to walk with the other feet.
I must have been wondering what I was doing,
how I could help a child I loved flee the traffic
of brutal marriage. Then the dog, free, that sick

look, somewhere, after a face that called its name.
I thought how wonderful would be a bell's faint
peal in that ear, then of Ron's vanished cat.
And Ron, who took the bell off, when that was that.

Failure of Fishing

To close the door on long days, to enter the welcome
broken club chair, magazines askew, plate
she has left waiting: I see my son and a white dog,
summer field like a lantern glow, only
it's my son's son, or maybe his son's
son, face hardly exposed yet
that will hang onto a man like a pond's smell.

Maybe that's all we get to keep, the half-seen, or
not even that, walloping frog, a leaper,
literal's shadow, hum and bite at neck, place
where I looped my little light-test line,
talking for swirls of bass, saying oh hell,
be a big crappie, at least. Dusk
cooling so fragile legs stand, agree to sing again.

I can hear the friction rising from grasses, black
pressing down, doves peace-making, no breeze
but my breath trying to blow dark away,
wanting more time, and wanting
to squat there with my feet in the blood-warm
shallows, gaze fixed at the deep's edge.
Is it getting ready for me, or me for it? Then,

the smell of day cooling. I would ask where my father
was when he was a boy, in what place
he left to leave me here. I'd think of fish
he hooked, those that got away. Mostly
they wouldn't come to me. Still
moon trued my path from the hot field. Mouth
soft as a chair, plate-eye rising, home waiting in the dew.

Zydeco

The heat that day slimed the skin,
    dogs and cats lay together, the shade
        found itself crowded with crawlers.

There was no water to be lonely with. Yet,
    in the Quarter no quit could come where
        dirt lay heating up, the smell of lovers

rising from that ancestry of brick, and slow
    recitations loosed from instruments none
        had heard before this day. A tale banged

by steel, kicked from naked toes, dragged
    from under saggy stoops, dropped in wisps
        hanging. The goldfinch spun, hung around,

when, late in that light, a swarm of flutter
    showed, butterflies, the sidemen said,
        on the way, like souls, to a cool house.

Before it was over you could hear
    each wing beating up and down, striking
        air until it rained, like brief, joyful tears.

Christmas Concert, with Violin

Christmas Concert, with Violin

The whoosh and rush of breath as we walked, film flickering
    in our heads, dark frozen in open mouths. Parking
lot massed with watchers, semi-circled, headlights splayed.
    A white boy, bloodied, knife-glint hung by jeans.
The downed blue shirt trying to rise, arms black as asphalt,
    pushed up a head gray-bald. Behind us others
leaving seats start forward but, here, now, we're first, alone.

Air, cold, stings. We're locked, standing, then someone waves,
    "Go on." People make gusts of crying terror, feet
scrape unseen like sleet at windows. All we know asks why?
    Soon we can't remember what we saw. We rehearse
colors, numbers, hurrying into the world. Traffic's a string
    of poinsettias. Stores, houses flare, Christmas lights,
gauds, fake deer, hope, joy, the stillness, now, seems to hold

under iron stars glaring down. You say, let's drive out, see
    what's waiting, an old habit. Somewhere a season
I forgot returns, a village where we thought danger couldn't
    come. I taught the girls people wanted out of harm,
beset them with unworried books, safe, alive, bound in by all
    we might design to avert time's boredom and flash.
We were lonely, you living for babies we made, me for words

I heard as dark's breath-whistled rage to live. Stalks, we bent
    in black dirt where a scouring wind heaved, just
ourselves to lean on, fear rattling us with it all. But what is all?
    By October the peeling sycamore hung bare.
November rain clenched each step. Blank-eyed owls drove in
    mice, mouths gulped close we almost didn't hear.
We stared at news, coiled like field snakes inside hiding walls.

We'd wake feeling half-touched by something prairies kept.
    Christmas came, its cold, short day like a nail,
cows turned faces flat, slants of ice hurled at every surface

until each tree, roof, bush seemed lost inside
glazed mirrors. Too late, I said, to find a church. You cried,
        wanting mass, and I broke loose the frozen
car, complained we'd never see again a godforsaken college

town where nothing seemed alive. I remember we wrapped
        the children in your father's old army blankets,
checked the Kansas City weather one more time: awful cold,
        clear, high stars, a chance of change by dawn,
radio's hymns rolling over, tacky Christmas tunes belched
        by drunks for joy. But where churches hung
profiled at horizon no door swung, though I pushed or knocked.

No people knelt, no prayer held in babe's mouth domed that
        sky, no bells shimmered. What had we done
so wrong we were left to ride in the miles of miles of miles,
        lured by a faint north star, like fools not knowing
what might turn murderous as air itself. Lulled by hot blow
        of Ford heater, children slept, we spoke softly,
hearing tires rasp the black pavement, bringing back those

faces that had, once, leaned down to love us, acrid powders
        mixed with whiskey, filling rooms we were
never afraid in. We drove, not thinking we saw no lights
        of passing cars, no important sky-glow or
tiny village gas pump with faint illumination. Crosby's voice
        broke through every turn and each switchback
teased us on. Still, we started whispering what might happen.

Colder than ever, night scared us with thickets of clouds, fog
        we'd roll upon like sudden herds across the road,
thick ropes of moon occasional now. We turned to go back
        but found no back, could not remember this
way we'd never been, a looping country way, tractors nudged
        under sheds so nakedly alone it made us
colder to look, fields far and leveled full of shined blue spill

that seized each separate house in chill, yet bewilderingly
　　each lit up a festive scene that seemed to carry
miles to the next place, road like a thread. But each dark roof
　　to us more fear, no sign of life up thin rutted
drives. Where were they all, why not here, games clicking at
　　boards, drinks poured, someone snoring as
darkness stayed desperate somewhere else? Then no houses.

We came to an intersection sprinkled with glass, two roads
　　going nowhere, no sign, no dwelling, business,
landmark, even tree. Then in headlights came three coyotes,
　　weird gray shapes, lean with noses down where
road ran, ragged fur riffling like the hair coats of travelers
　　in dreams, so intent they never looked beyond
whatever mission held them. "Look at those guys," I whispered.

They took the road oblivious as saints. Soon flecks of ice
　　like metal shavings, then blizzard. We followed.
Snow spooled, slammed, like treachery, hiding those shadows.
　　As I gripped the unknown way, snaking, we'd
see them in and out, crossing a creek, clattery bridge, the new
　　milk-blue on their backs like royal robes. And
then we saw the eerie flame-spurt like blackened paper's hole

where, words gone, the unexpected comes burning through:
　　fire like redemption in the fear-ridden heart
of the wanderer who, still, denies he's lost. Near now, first
　　tongues of yellow steepling to orange, spires
rumbling toward stars that must have been spinning somehow
　　too low, the shining glints of rock not for us.
Blind to my faults, afraid, hurtling through white, I skidded

until I saw a fume of wood's ashy pieces churning upward,
　　clots of smoke that boiled to snow, spun fields
to clouds of geese. I slowed. People stood, bundled at bonfire,
　　smoke like a comforter mantling them. I came

among a crazy quilt of cars shouldered close, pick-ups, even
        Winnebagos strapped with, maybe, the gifts
tomorrow would surely bring. Past all, a country church unlit.

"No heat, no power," a voice said. But we'd come too far, so
        babies hefted, we stepped up like quickened ghosts
through two tall doors, past vestibule where shivered those
        not quite in or out of the wood's bitter, hanging,
raw scent. Pews full, we took a stair. The same, but there
        two black ladies in straw hats the word big
can't cover scootched close and waved us down beside them.

Maybe nothing else could hold the fecund beauty of those
        bloom-blistered brims, roses like a Botticelli
babe's, a garden we could almost smell. Around us, below,
        faces flared with gold candle-glow, walls alive,
ceiling stuttered with little shapes like spirits. Some, you said,
        like fearful dogs. People watched, and I saw
none here were white but us. Then I heard the blast of song.

Nothing in that voice sounded like us. Do I say it was black?
        Each repeated every word looming first from
a sudden shade in a thick-furred parka at the altar. The preacher,
        long-nosed, toothy, hand-nails catching candles,
clawed the room and drew back howls of notes. So still we
        sat I felt my jazzy Baptist youth bob up, renew me
until I sang too, no sense I was wrong in a right place, as friend

Hugo wrote, a poet, then a finer thing opened: a choir of elders
        filed out of the dark, candles fisted, and pitched
up tunes I'd once sung in school, but never this woven wobble
        of phrasing that swirled about us like sweet heat
filling the whole wooden hall. Our two black ladies, bookends,
        from each outswelling mouth made sound of oboe
or maybe French horn, felling us to awed silence. We marveled

at each big bonnet urging us with shy touch to dip in the spirit
    now a river all were bobbing in, and nothing
to keep us from standing up to belt out whatever boldest
    blood desired. One kid each we stood and so I
tried their song, growing it with all I was until I felt nothing
    might be better than this grace. But then only
silence, me still singing. Oh, I heard the preacher's low growl,

and great doors whined back, a wind's withering whooshed in,
    candles sputtered out, the whole place sank to
blackness like a hog pen where coyotes crawl. Forward we
    leaned in small rustling at the rail. We feared
to breathe, as of some danger that watched us, one congregation
    pinned by what we couldn't yet see, but felt
a kind of massive heartbeat, too, like a wind that buffets inside,

a panic pumping our chests as doors, grating, closed. All gasped
    audibly, the general insuck of breath shuddered each
wickflame, and then rising bow-struck chord of violin's notes
    sliced from corners everywhere, bent, and went up
like angels climbing, veered, whirled, dipped, catapulted, leapt
    to double, treble heart-stroking sound that soothed,
then fell, stumbled almost, almost the sidewalk smack of flesh,

or slap on water suddenly too deep, the clinging to renew, climb
    up with some force not counted on, surge, soar,
drag, round, rebound, until the feet in my shoes could not keep up
    their stillness, and loudly tapped. We heard that
most astonishing and lovely lave of grace, as if the soul sang forth,
    the altar—I can't say exactly how—bursting the dark
with more candled light like a fury of sun's many colors, so we all

cried *Oh* in single breath, as if it were the word of perfect praise.
    Alone, there stood this girl, caramel candled, her
willowy torso swaying in white fur to make each note not like any

ears had ever known, I might have said, except a soul
poured all this composition down, didn't she? What joy, I imagined,
    to take from airy nothing a language to embrace all
the heart's hunger. We couldn't let our gaze go from the child

touching, turning that burnished wood more motherly, the strokes
    of bow breeding a kind of slowed, different time
where we floated up, on each single note buoyed. I saw her shade
    loom across the cross-hung wall, twice higher
than any among us, on either side the shaggy-coated elders stiff
    with night, behind them the cadres of pageanters,
three dressed to be the Magi, one, smaller, the world's infant boy.

We could see the breath of song crowding out the room's cold,
    and were not cold, the close press of two great
ladies angling us to the violin's trip along the far edge of a giddy,
    joyful run. Then, as if she knew all we could bear,
she drew a last long weaving embrace and backed into a buckling
    glitter to vanish, candles woofed, in yipped amens.
None then, or after, said her name or what brought her to spend

that holy night playing for the lost, or what tune it was, and little
    we could guess of ladies who led us where the road
went home, snow that fused its white with blackness we were in
    less thick, then a streaked gray sheet like a shroud
on all, and tracks the blind could nose home by. Now each year
    she plays in our heads, that angelic wailing cry
that makes us wonder if she's loved well, has kids, had dreams

yield all she needs, or found a dark way that's endless when alone.
    Of big-brimmed ladies who now lie stiff and long
in best silk dress, in frozen feet of dirt, who held off icing dark
    and warmed we wanderers, I make this tale.
Of words that will not save a single life, of steps that tap and go
    where music comes to salve the fearful heart,
we dream. Let's cruise and look, you say, as if to find again what

that night made us hear, the heavy flesh that breathed us for a time
    its own, and raised us to grace some have and give,
though it doesn't always work. Remember how they urged us in,
    all bonnet and perfume and teeth and big hug-to?
And what's knifing wind or blind-out weather to that? *Get up!*
    Sing! Tongue and violin cried. We did. Driving lost,
headlights ablaze with luck we were—remember?—alive again.

Photograph of a Waterman, Bull Island, Virginia, Circa 1970

In my office I knot my tie before him,
the expect-it-all look of his left shoulder
a fighter's, skin of his nose and cheeks bleached,
except for liver scars, and the deep, open
mouth caught like a fish about to speak, and about
his runny eyes shade of hat is back-tilted.

Behind him the 100-foot pier spills to tilted
buy-house, money's mounds of oysters opened
before memory. He's lifted—frail arms, shoulders—
years of crabs, fish, whatever swam before him,
wrestled boats, mud sucking it all back. About
ten yards right is another pier, its bleached

fish-house keeping men he can't abide, shoulders,
necks cocked in pride, backs turned. He's walked there, bleached
sun the same, but theirs a different world to him,
old insults rotten as fish and the tilted
men who limp past same roads, same marsh are opened
doors he can't go through. He's thinking about

blood, names, words, maybe, way his face, tilted
to see what you'll hiss, can't lie and won't open
that dark gaze, as sure as burning dusk. Bleached
bay slick and marsh stink hang at his shoulder,
Saturday, catch sold, sunken hull before him
(*one of them's,* he'd say), shells and scales about

all his shore keeps. What would they say of him—
last of a broke oyster knife? "O.K., open
up, shithead," his face says to the photo, bleached.
Two sons, his boat, storm-drowned, ride down his shoulders.
On the salt-rotted pier he's walked, tilted
sun falls finally down. Soon they'll talk, men about

fire barrels, the buy-boys hovering, who don't open
much their wallets. Faces fire-flicked gold, shoulders
flutter as words sting like black flies and touch bleached
deadrise sunk, woman old, fucking catch about
worthless, back busted, weak as a child, and him,
breath so bad you might die when he breathes, tilted

to offer his bleached face as he might for Him
he's pledged to, if croaker come back, and if bleached
shells rise that can't just any man shoulder open.

Hooks

I.m. Captain Robert Weaver, U.S.A.

I open the clasped metal box in my father-in-law's garage,
D-Day paratrooper, captain, many medals, long buried,
the bite of the barbed steel's lying there, snug in a drawer,
one hook fist-sized, like his cancer, smaller ones hidden,
cellophaned and sealed, ready to be used. Stored-away
smell acrid, a little like Cosmoline, things perfect as made.

Once I thought all I wanted when I went into the hazed
wooden alley of the hardware store was a fist of Eagle
Claws, hours spent guessing what each size would capture,
quiet aisle and hum of ceiling fan altered only by splash
of breaking voices distant in knobs or paint, saws or rakes.
I must have been a bad dreamer not to know how much
is never caught, how much survives, past control, to rot.

Here they are, in a dead man's dream-kit, perfectly laid out,
best hopes, wrapped in lock-away tape, outwaiting him,
thin, shadowy shanks and barbs no skin could resist.
For me they bring the oiled edge of men with bitterness
for what once worked, codes, reels, tools, hurt's weight
when I say we've run away, married, the line trembling.
"No," he says. "If you marry my daughter she's dead to me,"
who could not unplug what hooked him to his last breath.

A Dream of a Bat

We all think it's so easy not to be this man, or too hard,
because we'd not pick up a baseball bat and come
waddling, drunk, to the bar, showing off
for pals, then at blare of horn, words
boiling out of him outside. It wouldn't be like us

to catch the boss in his truck, still cursing a man for Christ's
sake, who wasn't at work as he ought to have been,
another of those days, long history, and he
after all could swing that old baby
still. Asphalt full of glass like silvery tears, blood

too, then silence like you never heard it, and little heads
of sparrows going off as if amplified, flinging
themselves ahead—what do they know,
he thinks, falling down? Plenty, he squints,
they know goddamn plenty, why they fly off fast.

He has to piss so bad, can't push himself up, so thinks
where do they go when they have to go?
The bat helps him up, its gouged,
scabby-scarred length useless as the dick
he always trusted, a weight he'll drag on home,

nothing the woman gets anymore. Why's it slippery?
Shade's cool—is it Saturday? He can clean up
the yard, haul to Goodwill, wait for
a drink like his father. Or swing
the bat at pine cones, work something out.

When he gazes, it leans into a boy's hand, fingers
picking it from a rack of its kind, cleats,
odor of his glove with neatsfoot.
By itself it has stood in darkness so long.
What must he do with anger that blows at him?

He has struck apples, rocks, gourds, and of course balls.
He can see the boy go in to buy it, then swing
at the face that fired him. A dream,
they say in the bar, the swing he had, who
rose up to piss, but darted out, like a bird at last.

Red Dress

I.m. James Whitehead

Just to get out of sun as rummagers do,
I walk into the Goodwill and kill time
while my wife shops. Big women who waddle
stand in shade-pools where a plus-size can roll
easy as carp. I pass dazed faces and face
east out of the late flesh-burning light. One
woman holds a red dress, eyeballing. I laugh,

but not too loud, her sly wink saying *Caught!*
and we sink deep in a moment of wanting.
Fire-fingered gold sequins drift at the breast,
silky fabric, shimmery T-shirt for wet moves,
it sways in ways a slender girl must yearn for,
but its too-little skin would howl and scream,
tear the heart if coiled nails tried pulling it on.

She grins, teeth creamy as buffed linoleum,
and how it happens I can't say but Otis
Redding comes humping through pipes overhead,
our pond-tub of shade shivers and off we go,
a manic, bopping, mid-aisle tango of hips.
That's how I remember a dead man's dance, pants
ripped, mistake of a floor-sliding tackler of

notes Jagger whoofed in a dirty ode. Jim, that day's
all-over joy still shakes me, and this woman wears
me and Otis like rain until, still alive,
I turn away, pass the aisle of cardboard palms,
the fruit stacks, heading for doors to the sun.
But stop and look back. Why didn't we know
how years of want swell us and keep us the same

wrong-footed dreamers? "Nietzsche, that's me," you
cried, your game-heart thumping its last. The way
this beauty quietly crumples and disappears
what her fat fist wads in her bag, tucking
it under all she has carried for so long, eyes
like yours not looking for any way out, moves
bold, right with light toe-ticking as she slides on by.

When death came for you, I grinned. And why not?
Huge pants splitting like a girl's lips in the dark,
you danced the air, your whole life breaking in
floor moves, feet feeling the force of all that
swelled you. Remember that girl, how you sang?
Summer drinks, dim rooms, a muse's swooshed red
we all tried, you the last and the best, big feet tapping.

Tongue and Groove

Forms a lock. But how does it begin in this world? The twig
falls, snaring another, and another, a storm's blackness
gathers and sends its will scudding down and over the quiet
niches of the forest, where a nest of barky remnants
holds, waiting it seems, and is then lifted, swirled away.

Like the afterlife. We never see where they land or in what shape.
We mimic what we can. We remember. We say *this way.*
The shadow man's fingers feel the groove. Fits to it
a piece of firm, now barkless wood, slender and pliant,
then into it, then deeper, snugly, and carries it with him a while.

When the wall stands, ugly and crude, needing its wind-cover,
the hand, after the night with love, fashions plank and rib,
wets for entry, slides, sees this cannot be easily parted.
Long years hold up the rich color, the vein-mapping.
Some like to sand hard, thinking to get back the early patina.

My wife from the first wanted to paint it brilliant cloud white.
Such an old look, such dour faces. At last I gave in.
The paper, medium rough, slid like a small hill of gravel
loosing the smell of pine sap. I could see the shadow
felling the tree, making the rib, the lock, nailing up forever

what would soon be lost in the sailing white, layered like mist
you cannot see through. The little nail holes puttied-in,
like eyes, slab after slab shoulder to shoulder, knots where
limbs grew, room like a snow-crypt. We live here.
Still, I know stains will rise some day, the lock split apart.

The Ordinary Animal

Yesterday a girl crossed Charles Street, late for chemistry,
dodging, almost, a truck hood, missing her test,
her step. The sun stuck to asphalt.
Who hasn't seen the little pool like shining oil?

Today carnations, stuffed animals, dolls, folded poems.
Why don't we make people follow the rules?
Why wasn't the truck driver beaten? The animal
biting at my heart is small, quick, ordinary.

Late today, or next week, the trash men, who sweep away
what is abandoned, will sing sex songs under
their breath. I have seen them steam,
carrying on. Animals playing, oblivious.

One of them takes a cracked flute, a wheel to his little girl.
Surely he cleans the trash first, the stains,
giving each toy a name she will love,
throw-aways not like anything in their beauty.

Leaping from the truck that screeches to a halt, young ones
mock him with plodding songs, glistening sweat,
bright chains their signals to the world.
They sing call-and-response, ready to play, to mate.

Sometimes the dead, greasy as cold pizza, touch him,
kicking his chest to a gasp. Before my trash,
lifting a typewriter, keys stuck, he bowed.
What kind of language does a poem want from me?

Birds razor the air with voices building rhymed rules.
The quiet is a room for all the outlaws
snagging and romping just as life wants. Oh
to be saved in the din so perfect that comes weekly!

Dry Cleaner

At the dry cleaner's I stand in line, my feet
shuffling weight from side to side,
impatience all over me while the woman,
light brown, with her Creole story drones on.
In New Orleans none would notice.
She's exotic in Baltimore, a dawn bird
everything hears. Even the clerk
leans into her tale, clucking softly. When
people behind me cough, she won't be
rushed. She's got her whole story to go.
Soon there's a man she never married,
her mother opposed, far away still, and he
went into a bar, wrong place, wrong color,
wrong words, maybe, a good man.
He'll never come away of there, not comin'
home, geraniums on the back porch,
and not replace the bad tire her Honda has,
who could always be telling her what time
does in the kitchen if she stand half
naked letting his dog go on out. So
let me pay you for him, give you money
because you is nice and I remember,
her nearly singing voice sighs. The sleeved
pants, two shirts hang on the brass ring, all
finished, unclaimed, the stiffened
stains gone away. The perfectly starched
cloth a redemption so beautiful
it might be the linen of royalty, but small
for a man two of us will think of as
sleep scuffs house walls like tide under a boat.
How nice they are, these women doing
the little one person can for another
which is, in the end, a wash
of memorable words that leave you standing.

Fireflies

You see them everywhere and hardly notice the one
cranking past as you pass on the sidewalk,
that mewling, watery eye, partly bloodshot, partly
focused on you, or some apprehension of you,
or, shrunken, one in the Giant self check-out line,
foul as a just-risen pig, in slippers, and now
the puzzled, warty face turns to you, and you're
helpless, stunned, the routine ordinary signals are
suddenly hieroglyphics, you're punching out
answers, your life savings gone, and a bug's winking.

Better, unquestionably, to walk faster, left on Main,
take the boiling sun on your back, still broad
enough to hold whatever comes next today.
That's the trick of it all, knowing you can,
without thinking, navigate, slide, cut quick
the way kids on front yards do in that smell
of mowed grass, sweat, youth, not dusk yet,
a tumbling brush of bone and skin only sweet
proof of no intent, intersection and angle, the right
desire of things as subtle as what fireflies mean.

Once my wife and I, following the girlish realtor,
opened a parlor door, brownstone dim, cool, two
bodies in pajamas pushing up in a musky bed
no one supposed to be there, husband and wife,
I've thought all these years. Their throats opened,
calls horrific as ungreased gears, dry pistons, us
already heeling out. Did someone later come,
explain who we were, snafus, that unlocked door?
Or did they lie, walls creaking, until dawn, bugs
at windows like words in their mouths, on and off?

Cumberland Reunion

To her last prom, the final high school reunion, I drove
my mother, arthritic, widowed, wanting to see
as we climbed Cumberland's hills, gray
men shuffling to work, coming home as
afternoon sun pressed hard over those
so few they weren't one class. Then up the broken
streets, cars lodged hull to hull, wheels tucked in,
garbage in gutters bricked the old way. *Few faces I know,*

she sighed, *Fridays here they start weekends early.*
Row houses block after block, and bars freckling
the dark solitudes, in windows neon come-ons.
I could see perched on stools a clutch
of darlings, heads turning as slowly
we passed, each one she might have refused,
a mirror's flicker, day waning, ball caps
soiled and low. Which one is he? I wanted to ask.

On we climbed until, puffing, she giggled and pointed
me inside. She wants to show me off, I thought,
sweating, and now, at jukebox, she twisted a little,
reciting songs, lines gone to war, sweet words—
until a raw floor-scrape of shoes, *Drink, lady?*
Then light we stood in so suddenly. One hawked,
stools spun, some old boys laughed back into tales

they couldn't escape. Smoke hummed from the hole
of each next bar, so we walked on. Here were trees,
she said, the river smelled, my room was too close,
I saw ducks ride away, snow came. Your father
wanted to go, so we went. Streetlights
flicked on. She seemed lighter now, heels
skipping, almost, over cobblestones. They'll see

your father in you, she'd said. Crossing B&O tracks
where they'd all been carried away, the dead
GIs, swells, ladies, the porters in black,
music I hadn't heard yet pushing them on
I imagined, sweetly powdered, the white heads
bending into the hotel where they had been
once forbidden to go, the shawled, slender girls

swaying as a tune needled them. In the deep blue above,
mountains like walls, stars loomed clear and boyish.
My heart ticked from going up Second Street.
Sweating, I thought how they'd be waiting,
the last ones, eyes made up, the first
glance of something they hadn't known,
big red hands reaching to them, like mine, fumbling.

Hawks on Wires

Along the two-lane asphalt that winds to the house
where my mother is dying, they dot the sky.
Always alone, even the littlest, heads untucked, eyes
calibrating like laser-beams, bodies like bolts.
Nothing their size can rise free from the earth but
must stay put in ditch-shadow, in tree-groin.
A swiveling gather of the head on its axle is able
to hold sun shaft or cloud step, and matches up
how far and how quick, its vectoring geometry
a gift of the nest, a gift of the air, without scruple.

*

The wires are like skin twists. They are quivering
like cello strings genius fingers, the notes I have
in mind faint before the birth of Jesus, before any
splash sibilant on the first beach, or the brilliant
spatter of blood-drip over pine needles. The rustle
of what is happening so the whole field knows
presses on me, as if the wires have been programmed,
players looking up, ready, even the road-kill deer.

*

Legs rigid, death-stiffened, cornea glazed and aqueous
humor already iced, gag of the doe goes with me,
Mozart on radio. Will prayers be heard? My wheels
strike nothing, a gust on tiny ears shudders for
small hawks waiting until God sings I want you
to send me mysteries in plain, weathered shapes.
So, whimpering, they start to fling themselves forth.
Below, muzzles cold, tongues needling light, scurry
like the unloosened spray of stars when wind turns,
a story opens, a mother's milky first voice begins.

Two Funerals in the House

I.m. Brook Eley, Randolph Eley

1.

First death the boy's, sent home from sea's pall,
lung-drowned, breathless, who'd run Virginia hills
where he lived from rise-up and step. Neighbor said
he'd be naked in their door, hand out-held,
got a tookie, please? Too young for hill-grave,
no son, no widow yet, just the gold, gay
foreign girl who couldn't now say a word,
leaning on the father, and he onto her,
hymns soft, townsmen in the Methodist mew
with classmates standing, suits, t-shirts, the raw
ones out of work, faces wanting a smoke.
His big toy discharged in the shade, red truck
the rushed rain filled up, and leaves, and high dark.
He'd never have come home, the heads nodded.
Nothing here but mountain. Leaf-turn and lead.
Later, the preacher's blurt, laughs, a shudder
of Bushmill's, some hacked-off tales, ladies turned
in early for bed, or at least low-watt light,
the hum of talk from downstairs heaving at
why, why, why, and the way, sitting on ledge,
he, she, in last photograph, loomed, the edge
of valley deep behind defining falls.
To see him stand on stone's slippery will.
Or mic in hand, egging the dance on, that time
his brother married our girl, was to rime
his booted silver toe-flare, sizzle of
late cigar, father's pride, a goof of love
turned cherry bomb, then the father withdrawn
in house-dim like a hull moon-bobbing. We saw
the truck drown in black rain, the body propped
like a celebration, plug pulled, music stopped,

his electric face jokeless now, fixed, chalked.
The sun rose quiet where he was, suddenly, not.

2.

The father next, good man, gold chained, racks
of shirts, ties, shoes, the haute couture of Saks,
a keeper. Designer suits, lapels turned
too thin, too wide, nothing useless. Fair-skinned.
Unfurled, had the heady eyes of red-tail hawk.
Laughed like a Mason, believed, hand-shake
a life promise. Steady pour with long nose
of bottle, would dance, play fiddle (not well), sloped
by law, and the Lord's work, firm self, souled.
Would argue any side, send a man to jail,
buy him lunch, or write letters of petition—
murder wants mercy, your Honor, but convict
not his innocents who need help, Sir, and favored
travel to teach the virtues of home. Was said
to bet his young sailing son circled the globe
before thirty. Wrong. One son left alone.
We ask why what happened happened to them?
On back porch kept court, no answers offered, hum
of goldfinch like breath through summer's gum
leaves, a thistle-tube hung. There would shy
up glance to mountain's shade, as if blank eyes
of Jesus, waiting, watched. Weak, motioned us
to lift to lips his iced-tea glass (but not tea!)
because, by then pain-clotted, past words, he
could not. So I held that glass, took up the slack
of that arm that had cradled wife in black
three months back, the girl, the other son,
our daughter, the new child—arm of stone,
why that one? arm of good sinew, of bone,
arm that waited to serve and to play—why?

Arms slack as sleeves, content, he would die
trembled hard by bird-song, a man soon
saved, he said, no questions left, glad for broken
grips of friends come to sing, play banjo's tune.
I'd have worn a chain to save him. Jameson
poured, I drink to his grin, who only joked
he'd need new suits, bright ties to wear in the end
to honor that courtly life, that goddamned boat.

Glasses

The shoebox in my closet, mausoleum of frames, lens
cases, a round gold pair, antiques, templates slight as ghosts.
Wearing these, I saw George ferry in his dead father,
heart attack, so Billy, older brother, said burying the boat
needed one more. I wore them the day we rode over the bar,
George out of jail, me just barely twenty-two, the peeling
dinghy towed behind, sun a gas fire. In the V-notch prow
I felt salt crusting my face as we plowed and burst through
swells over bottom white as bed sheets, islands of green
sea plants waving in slow motion, choreography of tides
you can't see except by what they move. I saw everything
that swam and darted and burrowed there, then we curled
in a cove, its hummock cradling buried hulls canted as if
in forgiveness, ours next to be sunk. It was supposed to be
easy, we'd ram the slim twenty-footer in the narrow squinch
of shallow water between two already gutted, so far gone
thieves would find no brass screw, no wheel, no painted name.

I was supposed to putter behind, deliverer where a hole was
chopped, dinghy's once-drowned stuck throttle eased like
a latch, ferryman to those souls begot by the departed father
the soon-to-be-dead boat buoyed in and out forty-four years.
But when I pushed, it jammed, water holding on, and rust.
Gently at first, they called to me, then in hoarse commands
like those of Achilles watching the spirits of comrades fly off
in specks of blood, then George firing his old man's pistol
more or less at me. Ripping a knuckle, I snapped the petcock
off, bow lifting with a roar, the hull vaulting forward, rolled
side to side as I leaned to see tie-up stakes, glasses full of
spatter, maybe my own brains and pieces of skin, so like trash
I came finally settled all at once as if dropped from the sky,
water sloshing and chafing the way a man's terror will do.
Both brothers hopped in so the boat beat against the heaving.
"Son of bitch if I ever forgivet *you!*" George said. Billy glared.
I wanted to wipe my glasses but, soaked, I rode blindly in.

Today along the bar shore a cold scatter of boats, gulls high,
tacking in sun's way, cries the same as ever. Every face
follows the marsh cuts where the smell of gas mud makes
decaying is all it takes to call back a waterman's odor, salt
stink of bushels stacked, held up to the buy-man, then hot
whiskey, soft talk hours. Each splint of driftwood seems
somebody's bone floating off, in reeds the hulled, broken
gouge of handwork, wood smooth to the touch as a father's
pale brow in his box—they were supposed to hack out a hole,
two in tandem, me to ferry, but did not, unable to blink off
what happens to love. We wiped our glasses in a truck,
drank whiskey all morning, puttered back to lives on land.
Boat drifted. George died. Billy, unsleeping in a chair, rocks
watching the bar where what all's like scum in a paint can.
Years back cataract surgery for me, the smallest move of
fin or claw a ready text. Gold frames in a drawer stashed.
One lens an eye thumbed out. The other full of water shining.

A Drink for Peterless

The last I saw him, George, the mostly jailed son, was out
at the come-in dock and the father was the bag of goods
George was passing up to the long hands. Old, old heart.
Twelve children, one bed, one house, one boat. Homer,
the only woman he knew in the Bible's way, rocked for him
to get home, hurricane surge eased over the wood floor,
enough Billy, the other son, said it lapped at her underwear.

Peterless would shoot him a look if he'd tell that. The slug
of bourbon, sluiced in Mountain Dew, made his face red,
his hair white as foam over the bow cleat. One arm caught
in a pulled-up crab-trap snapped like bad chain. Happened
a Christmas snow. Got to get it off the boat, sure as hell
she'd sink, water's water godammit all. We had a drink.
Young, I called him Mister. They said "Peterless," quietly.

Billy said we'd all pitch in, drove three in front, three back,
old man like pimento cheese between two so pale fish
nosing would not stop to sniff. Didn't speak. Had a drink.
On the boat we made snow fly, shovels, handfuls, swirl
of brooms, him in the cabin, room for a gnome, watching.
Eyes cold as water where we pissed over side. You, said he,
you go to college? Same to each one riding back, car thick.

Not many, Billy says, who'd know every barnacle-raked
rock, current-suck, keel's peril. He did. Drank, got lost.
Never left, went nowhere. "College boys," Peterless spit.
Black suit, small in the silk box. Loved babies and ladies,
wine in water glasses, thin, wind-rawed. With this drink
I watch the jowly ones slide up, moor in corners, fists
curled at stiff Beams, room stilled for these gods of dusk.

Goose Blind

For Dee

Wild reeds woven to a small room,
dying tips brown-gold and whispering
in wind-rattle. Porter, whose farm is
bare, fields married to water, honks
as if the earth is talking, his old gun
hugged to him, his bone nose up
for two dipping fly-bys. They veer, but
glide around. "Mated pair," he says softly.

I think of us, forty years ago, side by side,
going south on 17, Dismal Swamp's
bogs all green lace because March is
done, April's warm inlet calls us,
because we lay on the sand, car radio
booming James Brown, joyful news.
At Nags Head Bridge we turned back,
just married, tiny boats half-sunk in marsh.

Shivering, wondering why I am here,
a guest among floaters over marsh,
chopped corn where oysters were, each
wet black eye that knows only rising,
falling with the sun's time, unafraid,
like you, once, saying let's go so far
years drift, pile up where all is surf,
roofs, the horizon we watch go dark.

Round and round the two fly, wanting
to eat, afternoon graying, wanting
to lie with the field's others, wanting
home's fixed, upcalling silhouettes.
On sky's long flow, like guests, pairs
slip from V-lines, tumbling. "They just
can't go on," Porter says, honking home's
urgent cries they seem not to want to hear.

Ode to Waffle House

Ode to Waffle House

For David Bottoms

1

A friend who believes he is coming to the end
calls me up, says let's have a drink, a few drinks more,
and talk about our vision. I say hell,
I can't get God to answer my call,
my cell spaces out like a mumbled prayer.
He says, let's talk about it, my friend, and oh hell.

It's dark, a weird red light's in the Moose Hall, dead
ice flickers in ditches and winter holds on
like ladies dancing with each other. No
jukebox eternally runs, nobody's songs go
past the last fork of the road, and home's
where coffee's cold as the front door handle. So

wisdom is, friend says, another splash of Jameson.
And why not a Waffle House, too. It'll do, I say,
as we stand near the driveway's edge.

2

After a while, our wives gone off to bed, the lies
we've been telling stand and take us out
prowling like old dogs. It's still dark, men.
This is the South, kingdom of interstates,
warehouses, guns, journeys, and the Waffle House
where you eat cheap and words still rate,

so we get in cars and trucks, we wave our hands
this way, vigorously, as if to someone who is dead.
Down here there is always one fifteen miles or less
either way, big yellow sign like the sun.

3

First thing, they hello you. That's good. Three sirens.
One's puckered, plump as an aging orange, lacquered lips.
The second, hair-bun skewered and raked by time,
grins wildly, gold cross at breast, third's
a dark shadow, tall in tennies, and on us
with coffee before our butts slide hard
where a god wouldn't waste an hour. We do. Then

fortune brings one more out of the chill: Hello, Buddy,
hail the three, all over him, and it's a good, friendly
triad all around, the rest of the grotto holding
not a soul this late, and outside a scrim
of untrod flakes is changing the dark to dream.

4

Soon we're hunger's very howl, and three maids milking
orders, full of banter and fun, cooking already
underway, because don't they know all
we want, their hustle singing with desire, gold
seeping from waffle press, juice swelling, and sweat
steaming up faces going from pale to glow, each
nailed-hand offering fill-up at cups we keep
pushing back empty, teasing like lovers, room getting hot.

5

You girls have been around, we croon. Oh you are wise! Bud,
each says, or Buddy, I'll be right here
you got a need. Ok?

We make them wink, nodding, like souls
who won't leave us while we grumble our no-mores—
no ties, suits, cubicles, adjustable mortgage, no weak-ass

shower, no breathed-in insects known to gobble
lawns, floors, truck's bumper and grille, no okra,
no fondue, no covered-to-the-grass
women of Iraq wearing IEDs, no dying
for goddamned George Bush or Bill Clinton,
dodgers as dirty as a mule's rear end.
Oh hell, no mule-God, no Dylan, no opera.

Each grace laughs, tickled by our every salvo.

6

All we are wanting is a moment of here,
a fine gold flare on our faces at last.
And don't these girls have plenty of that?
It's coming, Bud, hold on! Orange Blossom says, and sure

7

enough, it'll be smothered, covered, stirred, fried, syruped, laid
forth with a clatter by one shimmering like sunbeams,
a long looker, though as I say, we've been
in the nectar. Who wouldn't cry this is the good
we've longed for, pigging out as time flies,
telling lies about how we got here? That's why,

friends, I'd like to depict how flew my Trojan spear,
that moment in the past, how truth sought the breast
of mine enemy, who did pound his metric
foot on the battlefield, how came death's
defeat, the very thing I thrum for the girls
congoing in the galley while
with knife and fork I go on drumming, my best
urged on by high-fiving comrades! Oh horror
in the end, time's sandals that clack

every road a man takes! That's almost epic,

quips long-lashed Three, startling, so I add few go
in such footwear to Waffle House, mostly plain boots,
brogans, Nikes. I've been poetic. What
counts is style 24/7. Even when weirdness
like a sudden thong-sight picks you up why not
ask for meaning? That makes all three wigs sway,
the big yellow light brighter than ever. Talk on, say they,

8

words can turn hearers to knowers. No more silk-mouthed
say-er than do-er, Emerson writes, grunts one
leaning on chrome as on bower bed, two blink
like aging Supremes, faces lifted to glass,
gold headlights flashing east, dying South,
as if somebody's coming rumbling who matters.

Sweetie, I sigh, you got some hot sauce, please?

Where we've been replacements jockey up,
our dark lanes already open, slick new
combed-down, lotion-lathered rhymers squealing
up like eighteen-wheel wonders. Who were you?
they'll blink, as we get filled up one last time,
counter-rubbers aproned in that O Lord look
full-on as the high sign. How quiet we get, and why

not? Lady asks, More, Bud? End's near, friend jokes.
We all break up, it is all so funny.

9

That's when a cell phone starts ringing, the tinkle
of bells everybody slaps self to find, some

yo-yo calling to say are you saved? Or you coming
on home, sweet baby? We keep eating
the hot goods these girls bring to the table
as if forever faring forth, not just one
more ordinary night. Now's dénouement,

air kisses, hands clawed for small pay in pockets,
passing whiffs of old men as we step off—
Goodbye dearies bent over steeping utensils,
goodbye burnished fridge box and green
milkshake maker, goodbye tickets,
goodbye goddesses still whistling, it's the end.

10

                                    By separate cars,
in the long flow of dark floating off, in out-there's
birds rattling their livid call-me tunes,
in each black eye gone wide, in loops
a bald-headed swooper glides, I persevere.
Oh Buzzard, who sings to you today?

In my head I go home
charged up by the Waffle House trio,
one froth-sweet as orange trees, one mouthed
like Motown, still singing, third's tenny toes out
pirouetting the squeaky linoleum,
their pumped-up last howdies like torpedoes
of sun at my Goodyears, sky breaking to flakes
as each painted face lifts a puzzle. That's how

this dream leaves me at my stoop. Friend comes too, for
what is a tale with no friend to hear it?—
light fills the house, my dreaming love stirs,
the front door swinging when we go in and sit.

Soon enough someone says, Once upon a time—.
Pour the wisdom, I add, we'll get warm.

Hello us one more time morning of flared gold.